CHOOSING DEMOCRACY

Democracy and Other Forms of Government

Rebecca Sjonger

CRABTREE
PUBLISHING COMPANY
WWW.CRABTREEBOOKS.COM

T0019885

CRABTREE
PUBLISHING COMPANY
WWW.CRABTREEBOOKS.COM

Author: Rebecca Sjonger
Series research and development:
 Janine Deschenes
Editors: Ellen Rodger, Janine Deschenes
Proofreader: Wendy Scavuzzo
Design and photo research: Katherine Berti
Print and production coordinator:
 Katherine Berti

Dedicated by Rebecca Sjonger:
For Clara and Myles Beckner,
who are always up for an adventure!

Front cover: Governments are elected by the people in democracies to represent and serve on their behalf. Representatives often meet with members of other governments. Here, United States President Joe Biden and other politicians and White House staff participate in a virtual summit, or meeting, with representatives from Australia, India, and Japan in 2021.

Crabtree Publishing Company

www.crabtreebooks.com   1-800-387-7650

Copyright © 2023 CRABTREE PUBLISHING COMPANY

Printed in the U.S.A./072022/CG20220201

Published in Canada
Crabtree Publishing
616 Welland Ave.
St. Catharines, Ontario
L2M 5V6

Published in the United States
Crabtree Publishing
347 Fifth Ave
Suite 1402-145
New York, NY 10016

Library and Archives Canada Cataloguing in Publication
Available at the Library and Archives Canada

Library of Congress Cataloging-in-Publication Data
Available at the Library of Congress

Hardcover: 9781039663312   Paperback: 9781039663800
Ebook (pdf): 9781039668232   Epub: 9781039685635
Read-along: 9781039686120   Audio book: 9781039668720

Contents

Introduction

Modern democracy—the type of democracy now followed in about half the countries in the world—was established less than 250 years ago. Most modern democracies are liberal democracies**.**

They first developed in the 1700s and have evolved and changed over time. Some have become more democratic and some less democratic. Democratic systems differ from place to place in the world. A system is made up of parts that work together to meet common goals. Governments are systems, for example. Some are small, such as a student government in a school. Larger governments run cities, states or provinces, and countries. They are led by **politicians** assisted by the **public service**. They work together to make and uphold laws and customs.

Democratic Processes

Democratic governments worldwide depend on democratic principles and processes. A principle is a value that guides how things should work. A process is a set of steps taken to meet a certain goal. The right to vote is a central principle, as well as a process, in a democracy. In some cases, it is simple. People in a group can vote by raising their hands. Other votes are more complex. They involve many systems and people. Find out about other important democratic processes on page 14.

Elections all serve the purpose of selecting a person or an idea.

The word "democracy" also describes a place, such as the United States.

Democratic Principles

Individual liberty, or freedom, is one of the core beliefs of liberal democracy. Everyone is free to make his or her own choices in a democracy. But there are limits to freedoms. Citizens are expected to act together for the common good. These are called responsibilities. A high value is placed on respecting human rights. These are the basic freedoms and privileges that every person is born with. One key liberal democratic principle is that all people have equal value. They should have the same opportunities in life. They should also follow the same laws. Another right is being protected against discrimination. This is the poor treatment of a group or individual that is based on things such as race, **gender**, age, or disability. Modern democratic ideals put emphasis on being fair and **accountable**.

Disability rights advocates protest for equality near the British parliament.

Case Study

Brexit: Leaving the European Union

In 1973, the United Kingdom (UK) joined what would become the European Union, or EU. The EU is a political and economic union of European countries, with its own law-making **parliament**. Being part of the EU allowed for easier trade and travel since the 28 member states were given preference over other countries. Over time, some people in the UK felt that being in the EU had more problems than benefits. They thought too many people from other parts of Europe were entering the country for work, for instance. A referendum was called in the United Kingdom in 1975. A referendum is a kind of vote that poses a single question to settle a major issue. Citizens were asked if they wanted to stay in the European Union. Sixty-seven percent voted "yes." Those who wanted to leave the union were free to keep voicing their opinions. That is because democracies allow for **minority** points of view. The "British exit" issue became known as Brexit over the years. There was never broad agreement, or consensus. However, in 2016, another referendum was held. Just over half of the voters wanted to leave the European Union. This slim **majority** won the decades-old debate. The country left the union in 2020.

EU states include 447 million people across Europe. It functions as a single market.

ICELAND
NORWAY
FINLAND
SWEDEN
ESTONIA
LATVIA
DENMARK
LITHUANIA
IRELAND
UNITED KINGDOM
NETHERLANDS
GERMANY
POLAND
BELARUS
RUSSIA
BELGIUM
LUXEMBOURG
CZECH REP.
UKRAINE
SLOVAKIA
FRANCE
AUSTRIA
HUNGARY
MOLDOVA
SWITZERLAND
SLOVENIA
ITALY
CROATIA
ROMANIA
BOSNIA
SERBIA
MONTENEGRO
KOSOVO
ALBANIA
MACEDONIA
BULGARIA
SPAIN
GREECE
TURKEY
PORTUGAL
MALTA
CYPRUS

Many people in the UK still opposed Brexit after the 2016 vote. They demanded another vote.

Ancient Greece had direct democracy—for adult male citizens only.

Direct and Representative Democracies

Ancient Athens in Greece created an early form of democracy. Adult male citizens who were not enslaved voted in person on laws and how to run the **city-state**. This way of making decisions is called direct democracy. It is impossible in places with large populations. There are more than 200 million voters in the United States. Canada has almost 30 million voters. These countries and many others are representative democracies. Voters choose who will speak and serve on their behalf. The elected government leaders represent the citizens. This book begins by exploring how this looks in North America. It also describes American and Canadian democratic processes and values. Then it moves on to global examples. Finally, risks to democracy are introduced.

Direct democracy is still used by smaller places and groups.

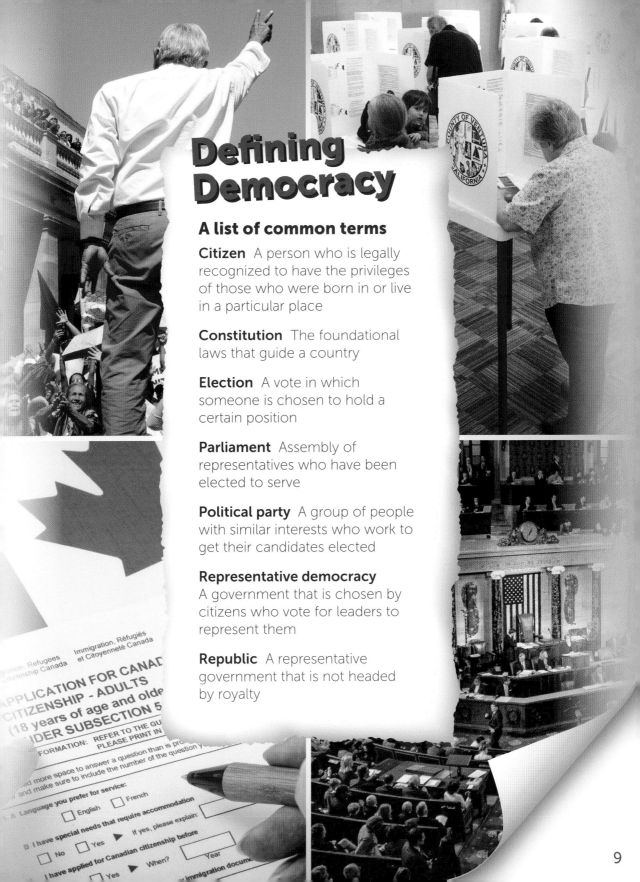

Defining Democracy

A list of common terms

Citizen A person who is legally recognized to have the privileges of those who were born in or live in a particular place

Constitution The foundational laws that guide a country

Election A vote in which someone is chosen to hold a certain position

Parliament Assembly of representatives who have been elected to serve

Political party A group of people with similar interests who work to get their candidates elected

Representative democracy A government that is chosen by citizens who vote for leaders to represent them

Republic A representative government that is not headed by royalty

CHAPTER 1

American and Canadian Democracies

The United States and Canada are constitutional democracies. They both have a set of leading laws called a constitution. These laws outline the government's roles, powers, and responsibilities.

A democratic constitution applies to and protects every citizen. It can be amended, or changed. A majority must agree on any change and follow strict rules. The Constitution of the United States was written in 1787. Twenty-seven amendments have been made since then. Canada has a partly **uncodified** constitution. Instead of one formal document, it is a collection of acts, or laws, and traditions. These include the Constitution Act, 1982, and the Canadian Charter of Rights and Freedoms. Many of its customs are borrowed from Britain.

Alexander Hamilton was one of the Founding Fathers of the United States. He is shown here writing a draft of the constitution in 1787.

Check It Out!

Constitution of the United States:

**www.archives.gov/founding-docs/
constitution-transcript**

Canada's Constitution Acts

**https://laws-lois.justice.gc.ca/eng/
const/const_index.html**

Artist John Trumbell's painting Surrender of Lord Cornwallis shows British forces surrendering to American and French forces after the Siege of Yorktown (1781) during the American Revolutionary War.

American System

Canada and parts of the United States are former British territories. American **colonists** declared their independence in 1776. Later, they defeated Britain in the American Revolution. The new country became a **republic** with a presidential system. The head of state is the highest representative of a country. In a republic, that is usually an elected president. The American president is also the head of its government. The position holds a great deal of power. To prevent its misuse, roles are divided among the president and other government leaders. For example, the president can approve or reject new laws but cannot introduce them.

George Washington was the first president of the United States of America.

Canadian System

Britain's **colonies** in North America were joined together in 1867 to form Canada, a **dominion** of the British Empire. The British monarch is Canada's head of state. A monarch is the highest-ranking member of a royal family. The amount of influence a monarch has varies from place to place. In Canada, they give their power to the elected representatives. The Canadian government is a parliamentary democracy. The head of the government is the prime minister. This is the leader of the political party that wins the majority of **ridings** across the country. Minority parties have control, too. Parties can work together to hold a no-confidence vote. If they win the most votes, it forces the government to hold a federal, or national election. The practice keeps leaders accountable to voters and other politicians.

Think About It!

The head of state often has ceremonial **duties, while the head of government runs the country. Do you think these roles should be combined? Why or why not?**

Queen Elizabeth II shakes Canadian Prime Minister Justin Trudeau's hand. The queen is Canada's head of state. She is represented by the governor general.

Municipal	State/Provincial/Territorial	Federal

Federal Systems

American and Canadian governments use the federal system. Three levels—federal, state or provincial/territorial, and municipal—work together. The municipal, or local, level includes towns and cities. They are often grouped into counties, districts, or regions. Mayors, reeves, and councillors are some of the elected representatives at this level. They manage public services such as police forces, city planning, water and sewage, parks, and libraries. States, provinces, and territories have authority over local governments. A governor leads the representatives in a state **legislature**. A premier leads in a province. This level makes decisions about education, licensing, overseeing local governments, and, in some places, providing health care and other major matters. The federal government oversees things that affect the entire nation. Voters elect leaders for all three levels. Citizens decide who best represents their views on local, state or provincial/territorial, and national issues.

Federal governments, such as the Treasury Department in the United States, print money.

The state capitol building in Austin, Texas

City Hall in Toronto, Ontario, Canada

Jury members are chosen from the community to hear the facts in a case. They then cast votes to determine the fate of people on trial.

Participation and Processes

People must participate to keep democracies strong. Adult citizens are expected to do their civic duties, which means taking part in processes such as voting, paying taxes, and serving on **juries**. Americans and Canadians of all ages can also protest and **petition** their governments. They are able to contact and even challenge the leaders who represent them. They may support political parties, too. Political parties are groups whose members share similar interests and goals. They work together to get like-minded people elected as government representatives. Young people can get involved in political parties, too.

Voters are given privacy to vote.

Think About It!

Have you ever voted in a student election? Which factors influenced who you chose to represent you?

Party Politics

A democracy needs at least two political parties for voters to choose from. The Democrats and Republicans dominate American politics. Many other smaller parties exist, but they are not popular with many voters. Five parties were represented in the Canadian government in 2021. Most of the power was held by the Liberals and Conservatives. Third and fourth parties are important in Canada because they can determine the fate of an elected government in a minority parliament. Candidates are usually supported by a political party. People can run for election on their own, though. They are known as independent candidates.

RHINOCEROS

Anyone may form a political party. The Rhinoceros Party of Canada vows not to keep any of its promises if elected.

Free and Fair Elections

Holding regular elections is another democratic standard practiced by the United States and Canada—as well as other countries throughout the world. Democratic elections occur at set times as a way of assuring people that they will have a regular opportunity to choose their own government. American presidential elections take place on the first or second Tuesday in November every four years. Canada's system is more flexible. It must hold a federal election at least once every five years. The government usually tries to call for one when their government is popular with voters. It can also be forced into an election by a no-confidence vote (see page 12). States or provinces/territories, and municipalities have their own rules. Most citizens who are at least 18 years old can vote. All eligible voters are encouraged to take part in elections. No one is pressured to choose a certain option, though. Voters are given privacy to make their own choices. They hold a lot of power over their government leaders. Citizens' votes show whether they approve of what their representatives have said or done.

Adults from all backgrounds have the right to run for elections in the U.S. and Canada.

Voters in Virginia lined up to cast their ballots in the 2020 presidential election. In representational democracies, voting allows ordinary citizens to choose candidates who "represent," or speak for, them.

Political Culture

A healthy political culture is another key part of all democracies. This includes everyone taking part and sharing their views. Political tolerance allows for differences of opinion. A wide variety of ideas need to be heard. When people disagree, they should still show respect for each other. This can be a difficult ideal for people to follow. When politicians and voters insult or make fun of one another, they take the emphasis away from political ideas and make it personal. This can harm the public's trust in politicians and what they say. It can also lead to people not being willing to listen to the ideas of others.

Rule of Law

Another standard that is shared by democratic countries is the rule of law. This means that laws apply to everyone, regardless of their position in society, wealth, race, or gender. It helps prevent people in power—from government leaders to police forces—from abusing it. The rule of law also encourages citizens to do what is best for others. It helps a society resolve conflicts fairly and peacefully because the consequences for breaking rules and laws are made clear. The rule of law matters in democracies. Without it, people could be imprisoned without reason, or wealthy people could avoid or escape punishment for crimes.

Protected Freedoms

Individual liberty, or freedom, is a key feature of democracy. Many democratic countries, including the United States and Canada, have written documents that outline citizens' rights and freedoms. Many areas of life are included. For example, these countries separate the role and power of the church from the role and power of the government. At its most basic level, it means religion is a private matter and people can choose their own religious beliefs. Many democratic constitutions ensure that there is no state- or government-imposed religion. People are also free to live and travel wherever they want. They can choose which jobs they work at and how they give back to society. They are free to assemble, or meet with whomever they want. The media is free to report on the government's actions and help inform citizens. In a democracy, people should have the right to free speech. They can also object to other people's views. They cannot interfere with someone else's rights, though. These freedoms all help protect all human rights.

People are free to publicly protest in democracies. But there are still rules that govern many protests.

CHAPTER 2
International Democracy

Today, democracies are found on every continent except Antarctica—a territory claimed by many countries and administered by international treaties.

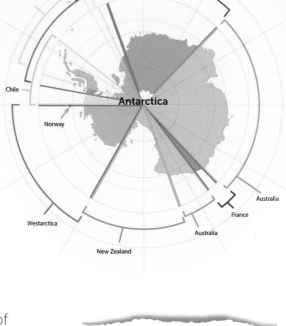

Democratic countries have many similar systems, processes, and values. Almost all of them are representative democracies. Most have written constitutions. The United Kingdom, New Zealand, Canada, and Israel have uncodified or partly codified constitutions. Some democracies have federal systems of government. Germany, for example, has three levels including state governments like the United States. Argentina has a provincial level like Canada has. Others, such as Croatia and France, have national and local governments. Those are called unitary systems, and the national government in these countries represents its citizens in more aspects of everyday life.

France's Senate is the upper house of the country's parliament (shown below). It has 328 senators who are elected as delegates of local governments. The French National Assembly is the lower house. Assembly members are elected directly by citizens.

Case Study

Switzerland

Switzerland is a rare mix of representative and direct democracy. Voters elect politicians to represent them. The representatives form a national assembly. Each year, they agree on a new president. This person acts as the head of the government. He or she is not the head of state, though. That role is carried out by a group of leaders. Switzerland has a federal system that includes 26 regions called cantons. Two of them still hold in-person voting, much like the direct democracy of ancient Athens. Citizens vote on national issues in referendums several times a year. This gives power directly to the people. In 2020, Swiss voters agreed to protect people from discrimination that is based on their sexual orientation. In another referendum that year, just over half of voters rejected a program that would provide lower-cost housing. That year, the COVID-19 pandemic disrupted the voting system for the first time since the mid-1900s.

Voting ballots are hand validated for a municipal election in Switzerland.

Constitutional Monarchies

Canada is one of 16 democracies whose head of state is the British monarch. These constitutional monarchies are also former colonies and territories of the British Empire which was once spread all over the world. A governor general represents the monarch in each country. This person carries out ceremonial duties on behalf of the head of state. The governments are usually parliaments that follow the British model. Some former British colonies have rejected constitutional monarchy. For example, Barbados, Guyana, and Mauritius all became republics after gaining their independence.

Mary Simon became the first Indigenous person to be the governor general of Canada in 2021.

The UK's House of Commons chamber is where the lower house of parliament "sits" and debates bills during government sessions. The British parliament has altered and changed over time.

In 2021, the island country of Barbados officially became a republic—removing Queen Elizabeth II as its head of state.

British Overseas Territories

All but 13 of Britain's former colonies are now independent countries. The 14 remaining are called British Overseas Territories and include mostly islands in the Caribbean and Oceania.

Bermuda
Turks and Caicos
Anguilla
Cayman Islands
British Virgin Islands
Montserrat
Gibraltar
Akrotiri and Dhekelia
Pitcairn, Henderson, Ducie, and Oeno Islands
Saint Helena, Ascension, and Tristan da Cunha
British Indian Ocean Territory
Falkland Islands
South Georgia and the South Sandwich Islands
British Antarctic Territory

British Overseas Territories

Royal Families

The United Kingdom is also a constitutional monarchy with a parliamentary government. There is no need for a governor general because it is the home of the British royal family. The huge size of the former British Empire means its monarchy is well known worldwide. However, it is only one of over two dozen that exist today. Japan, Lesotho, and Sweden, for example, are democracies with their own royal heads of state. The level of influence that monarchs have is different in each country. Many serve ceremonial or representational roles, but their power is limited by democratic constitutions.

Letsie III, is king of the southern African country of Lesotho. Lesotho is a constitutional monarchy but the king's role is ceremonial.

Queen Silvia and King Carl Gustav of Sweden. The King is Sweden's head of state, but the monarch's role is limited.

Presidential Republics

The United States set an example when it created its presidential republic in the 1700s. As democracy spread over the years, many countries followed its model. For instance, Costa Rica, Chile, and the Philippines all have presidents who are both the head of state and the head of the government. These leaders' roles are outlined in each country's constitution. There is usually a balance of power between the executive and legislative branches of government. An executive branch includes the president and a small group of department, or ministry, leaders. Elected members of government form the legislature. They work together to make laws and policies. These branches are found in most democratic governments.

Ram Nath Kovind, president of India

Diverse Forms

Governments can be set up in many ways. Some of their systems are quite complex. India is an example of a more complicated government. It is the world's largest democracy. Close to one billion people can vote there. The country has a federal system with 36 states and territories. India is a republic with an elected president as head of state. This person represents the country. It has a parliament that is led by an **appointed** prime minister as the head of government. This person leads the federal level of government. When a president and prime minister divide their responsibilities, it is called a dual executive or semi-presidential system.

Narendra Modi, prime minister of India

Women in Indian line up to vote with their voter identification cards. Sixty-seven percent of eligible voters turned out to vote in the 2019 general election. Women voters had the highest turnout rates.

Voting

The same democratic processes are carried out in different ways around the world. Voting is a prime example. Free and fair elections are at the heart of every democracy. The way that a country runs elections shows how healthy it is. Many governments have departments that manage the process. Set dates and fixed terms keep power from being abused. They also allow voters regular chances to choose new people to represent them. There must be openness when there are questions about voting rules or possible wrongdoing.

Required Voting

Many countries struggle to get people to vote (see Chapter 4 to find out more). In some places, citizens must vote by law. That is why Belgium has one of the highest turnouts on election days. Almost nine out of ten eligible citizens vote. Sweden's number is almost as high. Voting is not required there, however. Swedes are simply doing their part. In comparison, about one-half to two-thirds of Americans and Canadians show up to vote.

Taxes

Another important civic duty in democracies is paying taxes. Taxes pay for public services and benefits provided by the government, such as roads, bridges, drinking water, and old age pensions. Each place and level of government has its own tax rates. They are often a set percentage of things such as personal income, goods purchased, or value of land owned. The taxes are collected, and governments choose what to do with the money. Decisions are based on what is important to the citizens. Some countries have low taxes with fewer social services. Others fund more government programs to help citizens. For that, they must charge higher taxes.

Political Parties

Just as in the United States and Canada, all democracies need at least two political parties for voters to choose from. Many countries have multiple parties that represent people's diverse interests. It is common for one party to be more **conservative**, while another is more **liberal**. Other parties focus on one important issue. For example, the Green Party aims to protect the environment in a variety of ways.

The small island of Nauru has a different system. In that parliamentary republic, most of the politicians are not linked to a political party. They act on behalf of citizens. They do not need to represent a certain party as well.

Think About It!

The writers of the U.S. Constitution worried that political parties would divide the new country. John Adams, the second American president, said, "There is nothing which I dread so much as a division of the republic into two great parties..." How does having three or more parties help avoid the dangers of two battling viewpoints?

The tiny Pacific island state of Nauru has a 19-member parliamentary government. Most members are independent.

Legal System

The rule of law is the same around the world. The World Justice Project ranks countries according to how well they are doing with related democratic standards. This includes upholding equality under the law, fighting abuses of power, and holding governments accountable. European countries such as Denmark, Norway, and Finland lead the way. Canada and New Zealand often join the top ten. All democracies should have fair court systems. They are part of the judicial branch of government. This branch carries out laws made and passed by the legislative and executive branches. Most citizens are expected to serve on juries when needed. Jurors are randomly chosen and often have no legal knowledge. Jury duty is a common process in many democracies. However, Malaysia, India, and a few other places do not use them because of the potential for unfairness.

Political Culture

Everyone taking part and sharing their opinions is essential in a strong democracy. Lack of tolerance for differing points of view and little respect for minorities can be a problem. It is found in countries that have not fully embraced equality. In some places, for example, genders and social classes are discriminated against. Find out more about democracies that do not follow all of its principles in the next chapter.

Freedom of Speech

Citizens in democracies around the world should be able to protest and petition against their governments' actions. A movement called a Million Moments for Democracy in the Czech Republic is just one of countless examples. This group created a petition. It called for Prime Minister Andrej Babis to resign over his abuse of power. More than 400,000 people who agreed signed the petition. The group also protested. A protest in 2019 brought out 250,000 people in Prague. Freedom of speech and freedom of the press are also present in healthy democracies. When a government blocks traditional or social media, it goes against democratic values. Freedom of religion is another basic human right. A government that is influenced by church leaders may not serve the people it represents. Keep reading to find out more about what happens when citizens do not have these freedoms.

Think About It!

Which criteria do you think are most important for a democracy? Why?

Hundreds of thousands of Czechs gathered in protest against Prime Minister Andrej Babis in 2019. The billionaire president was being investigated for misusing government money.

CHAPTER 3

Flawed Democracy to Autocracy

The systems, processes, and values described in earlier chapters are democratic ideals. Each year, researchers for The Economist Group measure the levels of democracy around the world. In the 2020 rankings, only about 25 countries were full democracies. They uphold democratic principles.

For example, they respect citizens' rights and freedoms. Their elections are free and fair. Fully democratic governments are accountable for their actions. Fewer than one in ten people live in this kind of democracy. These countries are mainly found in Europe and a few other areas.

The United States was ranked #25 (7.92/10) on the list. It was listed as a flawed democracy for, among other things, low levels of trust in government institutions, politicians, and political parties.

Top 10 Healthiest Democracies

Below are the 2020 rankings according to The Economist Intelligence Unit*, which is run by The Economist Group.

1. Norway (9.81/10)
2. Iceland (9.37/10)
3. Sweden (9.26/10)
4. New Zealand (9.25/10)
5. Canada (9.24/10)
6. Finland (9.2/10)
7. Denmark (9.15/10)
8. Ireland (9.05/10)
9. Tie: Australia and Netherlands (8.96/10)

* The Economist Intelligence Unit researches democracy and is a part of The Economist Group, a private company that publishes *The Economist* newspaper. There are other organizations that produce similar democracy rankings.

Flawed Democracies

Many democratic countries do not meet all the criteria for being a full democracy. They are flawed democracies. Common problems they face include **corruption**, lack of citizen participation, and human rights abuses. About 40 percent of the world's population lives in one of those places. The United States slipped into this category for the first time in 2017. Its score was lowered in part by its voting system. Another issue was that its political parties do not work together well. American democracy is still much healthier than in many other countries. Mexican democracy is deeply flawed, for example. After gaining independence from Spain, Mexico followed the United States by becoming a presidential republic. Since then, the Mexican government has not always supported democratic ideals and processes. Mexico was only considered an electoral democracy in 2000. It has lacked free and fair elections, and citizens are not treated equally. There is still government corruption, human rights abuses, and threats to the rule of law.

On International Women's Day 2021, women across Mexico marched to protest against violence against women. They asked their government to impose tougher laws against the harassment, assault, and murder of women and girls.

Think About It!

What are some possible problems with collecting data from almost 200 countries each year?

Authoritarian Regimes

One-third of the world's population lives in countries that are not democratic at all. These places often have authoritarian systems. They may be autocracies or oligarchies. In an autocracy, total power is held by one person or a small group of leaders. An oligarchy is a group of leaders that share power. They are usually from the upper class, or those with a lot of money and power. These are forms of minority rule. The leaders do not consult with or welcome input from citizens. Dozens of authoritarian leaders have been in power for decades. The countries they control are mainly in Asia and Africa. They may use the title of president or prime minister. However, they do not represent citizens in the way that the American president or Canadian prime minister do. For example, Vladimir Putin has been in power in Russia since 1999. He has not allowed free and fair elections that could remove him from power. That means the Russian president cannot be held accountable by voters.

Russian president Vladimir Putin's rule has been called autocratic.

Military leader Omar Hassan Ahmad al-Bashir appointed himself president of Sudan in 1993. He held power until 2019.

Unlimited Power

Totalitarian governments are an extreme form of authoritarianism. They hold total control over citizens. People cannot express their opinions or fight for their rights. Turkmenistan, for instance, has been led by two totalitarian presidents since it gained independence from the **Soviet Union** in 1990. Some countries, such as Brunei, Oman, and Saudi Arabia, are monarchies, run by monarchs who have absolute power. They are above the laws set out in their constitutions. This is another form of autocracy. Their positions are often passed down through royal families. The rulers have no duty to represent the interests of their subjects. Military dictatorships are also authoritarian. Military leaders, like the ones who ruled Sudan for years, hold onto power through force. A coup occurs when the military overthrows a government. Other authoritarian governments are based on an ideology, or set of beliefs, such as communism in Cuba.

When President Saparmurat Niyazov died in 2006, Gurbanguly Berdimuhamedow took control of Turkmenistan.

The African country of Sudan has had two civil wars and many coups. It has been ruled by unstable governments and military rule for many years. In September 2021, the military staged a failed coup. Another one followed in October and eventually, the civilian prime minister was reinstated. The people of Sudan are not new to conflict or protesting for human rights and better government.

Case Study

North Korea and South Korea

Between 1910 and 1945, Korea was under the rule of the **Empire of Japan**. At the end of **World War II**, Japan was on the losing side of the war, and surrendered Korea. Korea was then occupied by the armies of the Soviet Union and the United States. The Soviets got the northern half, while the Americans took the southern half. They imposed two different governmental systems. The two territories were divided into North Korea and South Korea in 1948. Today, South Korea is a full democracy. It is a presidential republic with regular elections. The government represents its citizens and is accountable to them. They enjoy many freedoms, and their rights are protected. On the other side of the border, North Korea became authoritarian. Officially, it is called the Democratic People's Republic of Korea. However, it has the lowest ranking for human rights, political participation and culture, and the way its government runs. It has been governed by a family dictatorship for three generations. These contrasting countries show how different systems can arise right next to each other.

A fiercely guarded border separates North Korea from South Korea.

Hybrid regimes, such as in Bangladesh, could become more democratic over time. Free and fair voting is an important step forward.

A Nigerian woman shows her voter identification card, which was required for voters during elections in 2021.

Hybrid Regimes

Dozens of countries call themselves democracies, but they allow authoritarian practices. These are known as hybrid regimes. Many of these countries are in Asia, Central and Eastern Europe, and Sub-Saharan Africa. They often have constitutions but do not follow the rule of law. These places may not give power to citizens or protect their rights and freedoms. The level of democracy in hybrid regimes can shift over time. Some countries, such as Bangladesh and El Salvador, are trying to be more democratic. Haiti, Nigeria, and other countries are becoming more authoritarian. The next chapter looks at what happens when democracy is at risk.

Life in Autocracies

Democracies limit power by spreading it around so no one person is in control. This is flipped in autocracies. Citizens have very little control. Government leaders are free to use their power however they want. Human rights are ignored. Minority groups are vulnerable to attack. The rule of law does not exist. The government and military are above the laws. People can be put in prison without fair trials. They may be in danger if they share negative opinions about these leaders. The press is not free to report the truth. In fact, the media may be run by the government. Religious freedoms are often limited. Some authoritarian regimes, such as Iran, are theocracies. In those places, the government is controlled by religious leaders. Most authoritarian countries have only one political party, which always forms the government. Democratic processes such as voting are undermined. When there is a lack of free and fair elections, citizens cannot change their government leaders. President Paul Biya of Cameroon has been in power since 1982.

The official name of Laos is Lao People's Democratic Republic. The government is authoritarian and has total control over the media.

Think About It!

What might keep citizens from demanding their rights from an authoritarian government?

Change Over Time

Forms of government and levels of democracy change over time. The United States is the longest-running democracy. It is more than 200 years old. That is only a short time in world history, though. Most of the examples in this book have undergone changes during that period. Democratic shifts are always occurring. For example, the Middle East is home to many authoritarian regimes. The Arab Spring was a period of revolts against them. It began when Mohamed Bouazizi set himself on fire in December, 2010, in Tunisia. He was protesting police harassment. That led to protests across Tunisia. Zine El Abidine Ben Ali had been president for 23 years. He was pushed out of power. On October 23, 2011, Tunisians voted in their first free election since 1956. Tunisia is now rated as a flawed democracy, which is big jump from authoritarianism.

A Yemeni child gives the peace sign during street protests against government corruption in the western Asian country of Yemen in 2011. The Yemeni Revolution was part of Arab Spring protests that led to the end of President Ali Abdullah Saleh's 33-year rule.

CHAPTER 4

Risks to Democracy

The protestors in Tunisia brought democratic values and processes to their country beginning in 2010. People in countries nearby tried to follow their example. None were quite as successful, though. That does not mean people should give up!

History shows that the fight for democracy does not always go smoothly. For example, French citizens demanded their rights in the late 1700s. They created the Declaration of the Rights of Man and of the Citizen. They even forced King Louis XVI into switching to a constitutional monarchy. This was followed by more than a century of political challenges and disorder. The government changed forms often. France did not become a democratic republic until 1946.

King Louis XVI
of France

A Palestinian family holds posters with a question mark and the flags of Palestine and other Arab states.

Fighting for Democracy

Today, people fight for democracy in a variety of ways. Those who live in hybrid and authoritarian regimes take great risks when they protest for change. Even citizens in full and flawed democracies protest to protect their freedoms. They can also do it to help people in other countries. Everyone can work to hold governments around the world accountable for their actions. People living in democracies can urge their own leaders to take action. Researchers collect data to help educate people. Social media spreads this information faster and more widely than ever before. It can also spread **propaganda**, though. This information is meant to promote one side. It can be misleading. Helping democracy grow is everyone's responsibility. To prevent a place or group from being a democracy in name only, it is important for people to be active citizens.

Supporting other people helps reinforce human rights. These people in Toronto, Canada, are pressing for more rights for people in Afghanistan.

Threats to Voting

Even vibrant democracies can fail under the right conditions. For example, it could start to slip through problems with elections. Low voter turnout is linked to a variety of factors. In places with larger populations, fewer voters show up on election day. They often think their votes do not matter. When people are not well-informed, they do not know what the issues are and how better representation could help them. When the voting process is difficult, people may choose to not bother. Voter suppression is used as a way to stop specific groups of people from voting. Rules are made to discourage certain voters. They might need a certain kind of identification, or to vote at times or places that are inconvenient. The 2020 American election had all of these issues. Voters were frustrated when the process was not clear, or it was different from region to region. It seemed that the rules were not fair or the same for everyone. Many people did not trust the results. That will have an impact on future elections.

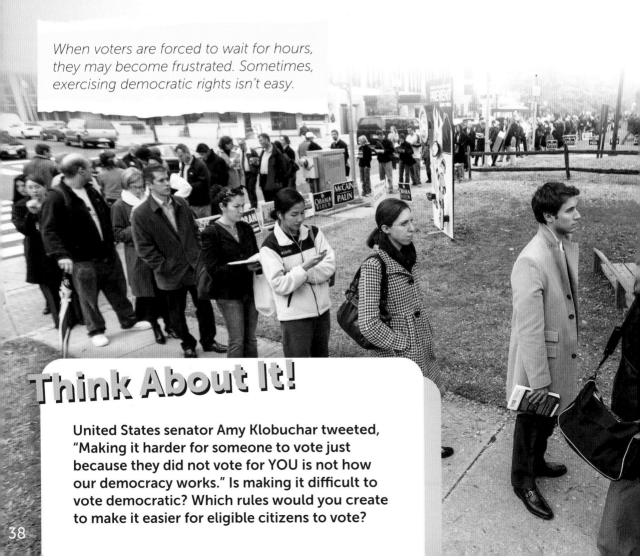

When voters are forced to wait for hours, they may become frustrated. Sometimes, exercising democratic rights isn't easy.

Think About It!

United States senator Amy Klobuchar tweeted, "Making it harder for someone to vote just because they did not vote for YOU is not how our democracy works." Is making it difficult to vote democratic? Which rules would you create to make it easier for eligible citizens to vote?

People from different backgrounds can work together to protect democratic values and human rights.

Other Threats

Democracy faces many other potential threats. These include political intolerance, citizens not staying informed, and politicians abusing power and not being held accountable. Discussing and debating issues can cause conflict if people aren't willing to hear one another's opinions and ideas. If the majority doesn't protect the rights of those who think or act differently from them, then some citizens are no longer treated equally. The rule of law is in decline around the world. This makes it easier for leaders to abuse power. It also means human rights are at risk.

Case Study

Freedom House

Freedom House is an American group that believes "freedom flourishes in democratic nations where governments are accountable to their people." In particular, they aim to help those who fight authoritarian regimes. However, they are also on the lookout for threats to existing democracies. One of the ways they do this is by collecting, analyzing, and reporting on international data related to democracy. These facts and figures allow them to spot trends. For example, their *Freedom in the World 2021* report noted that citizens of India had less freedom because the government limited dissent, or disagreement. Freedom House's resources help promote the rights and freedoms of people around the world. They work with local partners to help change laws, encourage democratic values, and end human rights abuses. To learn more about Freedom House, find the link to their website on page 45.

Protestors in India object to laws that make it harder for Muslim citizens to vote.

WHEN INJUSTICE BECOMES LAW, RESISTANCE BECOMES DUTY.

Members of the United Nations are trying to create a world that is fairer for everyone.

Protecting Democracy

Basic human rights, such as equality, no discrimination, and the freedom to express opinions, need to be valued—and protected. Most democracies have laws in place to do so, as does the United Nations. If laws are not being applied equally and fairly to everyone, citizens need to point that out. Not staying informed or taking action leads to abuses of power. Limits on power also help prevent abuse of it, especially by the government, the military, police, and other leaders. Issues with free and fair elections should be investigated and politicians must be held accountable. Allowing any of these things to go unchecked leads to flawed and failed democracies. Remember that citizens in democracies are expected to get involved and put the public good ahead of themselves!

Think About It!

Do you think that constitutions should be updated regularly to reflect modern ways of life? Why or why not?

**G20 ROME SUMMIT
30-31 OCTOBER 2021**

Active Citizenship

The United States and Canada are democracies with many similarities, but they are also very different countries. The same is true for the dozens of other full and flawed democracies around the world.

There is no single form of government that is the standard for democracy. From constitutional monarchies to republics, unitary to federal systems, presidents to prime ministers, there are many ways for democratic governments to run. Even their constitutions and other laws vary. Democratic processes are just as varied. Every country has its own ways for citizens to fulfill civic duties such as voting and paying taxes. Protesting and petitioning are used by people worldwide—and not just in democracies— to engage and promote change.

Think About It!

There is no simple definition of democracy because it relates to so many things. Has the way you think of it changed after reading this book?

The G20 Summit is a gathering of 20 major world powers to discuss issues that affect the entire world. It has been criticized for not including most of the world. Most, but not all, of the members are democratic countries or political unions.

Levels of Democracy

Criteria, such as free and fair elections, political culture, rights and freedoms, and the rule of law, are helpful ways to judge how democratic a country is. When places have problems with something as basic as voting, it is a warning that democracy is at risk. However, working together to solve the problems shows hope. A lack of tolerance or disrespect shows that people are not willing to work together for one another's common good. Another warning sign is a disregard for human rights, especially when minority groups are not treated equally. All citizens must be treated fairly. Leaders must be accountable to those who they represent, and voters must be able to remove them from power.

Take Action

Everyone can do their part to uphold democracy and democratic values. Citizens of healthy democracies can support people in places where it is weaker or does not exist. Young people around the world can shape what their future looks like. Getting informed is a great place to get started:

- Find out which government leaders represent your hometown and state or province

- Consider which democratic values are most important to you and what your own political views are

- Look online for more information about international human rights

- Research one of the places you read about in this book, and compare their systems to the systems in your own country

- Brainstorm ways you could contribute to the common good

- Spread the word about what democracy stands for and ways that it is at risk

Healthy debate and discussion can help you better understand democracy's benefits and failings.

Learn More

Build on what you have learned in this book. Use the resources below to research human rights and freedoms, government systems, and democratic processes.
Then use your knowledge to take part in democracy!

Learn more about the United States government:	**www.whitehouse.gov/about-the -white-house/our-government**
Get informed about Canadian democracy:	**https://bit.ly/3CFMdVP**
Find out about strong democracies:	**https://bit.ly/3FF8YLk**
Interested in worldwide democracy figures? Visit:	**ourworldindata.org/democracy**
Check out the work of Freedom House:	**freedomhouse.org**
View Freedom House country profiles:	**freedomhouse.org/countries/ freedom-world/scores**

Freedom House is founded on the core conviction that freedom flourishes in democratic nations where governments are accountable to their people.

Bibliography

Introduction

"Ancient Greek Democracy." *History*, August 19, 2019. https://bit.ly/3DNqPiK

"Brexit: Your simple guide to the UK leaving the EU." *BBC News*, July 30, 2019. https://bbc.in/30Vp58B

"Citizenship Education Resources." CIVIX. civix.ca/resources

"Defining Democracy." Facing History & Ourselves. https://bit.ly/3l5Eb2x

Doerr, Audrey D. "Public Service." *The Canadian Encyclopedia*, December 16, 2013. https://bit.ly/30V411J

Heslop, D. Alan. "political system." *Britannica*. www.britannica.com/topic/political-system

"Political system." *Science Daily*. https://bit.ly/3l2FbVc

Pruitt, Sarah. "The History Behind Brexit." *History*, June 20, 2019. https://bit.ly/3CKKj6f

"The road to democracy." The World's Children's Prize. worldschildrensprize.org/democracy

"Two Faces of Greece: Athens & Sparta." *PBS*. https://to.pbs.org/3xgoDha

"Universal Declaration of Human Rights." United Nations. https://bit.ly/3FHi7TH

"What Are Human Rights?" Canadian Human Rights Commission. https://bit.ly/31UtU2M

Chapter 1

"America's Founding Documents." National Archives. www.archives.gov/founding-docs

"Democratic Countries." World Population Review. https://bit.ly/30OPwgz

"Explore Our Country, Our Parliament." Parliament of Canada. https://bit.ly/3cH3gwc

Forsey, Eugene A., and Matthew Hayday. "Dominion of Canada." *The Canadian Encyclopedia*, November 7, 2019. https://bit.ly/3wNTS1j

Harris, Carolyn. "Constitutional Monarchy." *The Canadian Encyclopedia*, July 27, 2021. https://bit.ly/3HM5E2Q

"How Local Government Works." Association of Municipalities of Ontario. https://bit.ly/3r12Okv

"Introduction: The Democratic Process." Texas Gateway. https://bit.ly/3l4hRpN

"Knowing Your Roles: City and Town Governments Edition." MRSC, January 21, 2020. https://bit.ly/3xRtxR4

"Law and the Rule of Law." Judicial Learning Center. https://bit.ly/3HXVNXY

McIntosh, Andrew, and Stephen Azzi. "Constitution Act, 1982." *The Canadian Encyclopedia*, April 24, 2020. https://bit.ly/3l5Bpdt

Misachi, John. "Countries With Uncodified Constitutions." World Atlas, April 25, 2017. https://bit.ly/3HRq1Mi

"parliamentary system." *Britannica*. www.britannica.com/topic/parliamentary-system

Patrick, John. *Understanding Democracy: A Hip Pocket Guide*. New York: Oxford University Press, 2006.

"Presidential Election Process." USAGov. www.usa.gov/election

"Revolutionary War." *History*, December 16, 2021. https://bit.ly/3OXTqU4

"State and Local Government." The White House. https://bit.ly/3DLOoIx

"The American Voting Population." ArcGIS Online. https://bit.ly/3evJqFn

"The Constitution." The White House. https://bit.ly/3xekKcF

"The Rule of Law." LexisNexis. https://bit.ly/3l2FHm6

"What Are Democratic Processes?" Human Rights Careers. https://bit.ly/3hKAfTA

Chapter 2

Bognetti, Giovanni. "constitutional law." *Britannica*, February 27, 2020. https://bit.ly/3l22oXr

"Canadian election drew nearly 66% of registered voters." *CBC News*, October 22, 2019. https://bit.ly/3HYJ8Df

Dewey, Caitlin and Max Fisher. "Meet the world's other 25 royal families." *The Washington Post*, July 22, 2013. https://wapo.st/3zn3S4a

Drutman, Lee. "America Is Now the Divided Republic the Framers Feared." *The Atlantic*, January 2, 2020. https://bit.ly/3DOBHwy

Durkee, Alison. "As Barbados Drops Queen Elizabeth II, Here's Where Else The Monarch Is Head Of State." *Forbes*, September 16, 2020. https://bitly/2UfK0Ah

Foster, Sophie. "Nauru." *Britannica*, December 8, 2020. https://bit.ly/2ZjOIzq

Hutt, Rosamond. "These are the countries with the highest voter turnout." World Economic Forum, November 7, 2018. https://bit.ly/3zh5wDD

Lucchi, Micol. "This is how Switzerland's direct democracy works." World Economic Forum, July 31, 2017. https://bit.ly/3et6Yuj

"The Abolishment of Jury System in Malaysia." ALSA National Chapter Malaysia. https://bit.ly/3r82Rer

"The Swiss political system." SWI. www.swissinfo.ch/eng/the-swiss-political-system/45810052

"Which Countries Have Uncodified Constitution?" Maps of World, February 15, 2019. https://bit.ly/3zcY6B0

"WJP Rule of Law Index 2020." World Justice Project. https://bit.ly/2ZmocWc

Chapter 3

"Democracy Index 2020: In sickness and in health?" The Economist Intelligence Unit. www.eiu.com/n/campaigns/democracy-index-2020

Felter, Claire. "Africa's 'Leaders for Life'." Council on Foreign Relations, June 30, 2021. www.cfr.org/backgrounder/africas-leaders-life

"Global democracy has a very bad year." *The Economist*, February 2, 2021. https://econ.st/3oOOLvM

Gore, Hayden. "Totalitarianism: The Case of Turkmenistan." Human Rights & Human Welfare, University of Denver. https://paperzz.com/doc/8469088/totalitarianism--the-case-of-turkmenistan

"Laos." One World-Nations Online. Infogalatic. https://bit.ly/3nhdo47

Lynch, Justin. "How Sudan's Military Overcame the Revolution." Foreign Policy, August 5, 2019. https://bit.ly/3nGCtGf

Pilkington, Ed. "America's flawed democracy: the five key areas where it is failing." *The Guardian*, November 16, 2020. https://bit.ly/3iub5b4

Pruitt, Sarah. "Why Are North and South Korea Divided?" *History*, June 25, 2021. www.history.com/news/north-south-korea-divided-reasons-facts

Robinson, Kali. "The Arab Spring at Ten Years: What's the Legacy of the Uprisings?" Council on Foreign Relations, December 3, 2020. www.cfr.org/article/arab-spring-ten-years-whats-legacy-uprisings

Roser, Max. "Human Rights." Our World in Data. ourworldindata.org/human-rights

Shvili, Jason. "What Is Authoritarian Government?" World Atlas, March 25, 2021. https://bit.ly/3FN40fL

"What is the Arab Spring, and how did it start?" *Al Jazeera*, December 17, 2020. https://bit.ly/3CFhXKE

Chapter 4

"Expanding freedom and democracy." freedomhouse.org

Klobuchar, Amy. Twitter, May 10, 2021. twitter.com/amyklobuchar/status/1391920961402937347

Glossary

accountable Being responsible to others for your actions

appointed Assigned to a position or role

ceremonial A position that holds little real power or authority, but is important as a symbol for public or formal events

city-state A city that is also an independent state

colonies Countries or areas under the full or partial control of another country

colonists Settlers in a colony

conservative More traditional or, in a political party, more favorable to private ownership and free enterprise

corruption A form of dishonesty by a person in a position of authority that may be criminal

dominion A self-governing territory of the British Commonwealth

Empire of Japan The historical state of Japan from 1868 to 1947, before the modern state of Japan

gender The characteristics, behaviors, and roles that people associate with being female, male, or other

juries Groups of people (often 12) that are sworn to give verdicts in court

legislature The body of government that makes laws

liberal Ideas that conform to the political philosophy and belief in individual freedom, human rights, democracy, and free enterprise

liberal democracies Representative democracies based on liberal political beliefs that protect individual freedoms and the rule of law

majority The greater number, or a larger group

minority The smaller number, or a smaller group

parliament A legislative, or law-making, body of government in many democracies

petition A formal written request for something signed by many people

politicians People who are elected to office for a specific period of time

propaganda False or exaggerated ideas or information purposely spread to help or damage a cause, leader, or government

public service Services provided by the government and paid for through tax revenues

republic A form of government in which a state is ruled by representatives of citizens instead of a monarch

ridings Electoral districts

Soviet Union The Union of Soviet Socialist Republics, or USSR, that existed in Eurasia from 1922 until 1991

treaties Formal legal agreements between countries or sovereign peoples or nations

uncodified Rules that are not written out in a single source

World War II A global war that lasted from 1939 to 1945

Index

About the Author

Rebecca Sjonger is the author of more than 50 non-fiction books for young people. She still remembers which candidate she voted for when she cast her first ballot almost 30 years ago!